# *Cross-Fluence*

Stephen Campiglio

A Marco
Buona Fortuna!

March '18

Library of Congress Cataloging-Publication Data
Campiglio, Stephen Anthony.
Cross-Fluence / Stephen A. Campiglio.—1ˢᵗ ed.
p. cm.

1. Poetry

ISBN: 978-1-105-29114-2

Front cover art: "Emanation" © AJ Juarez

Back cover art: "Mountains in a Place You've Never Seen"
© Michel Duncan Merle

Photo of the Author by Roger Gordy

PRINTED IN THE UNITED STATES OF AMERICA

2012

First Edition

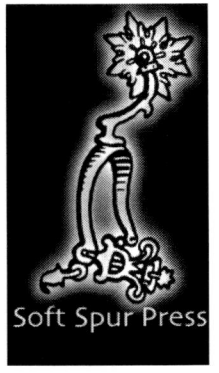

Soft Spur Press

Published by Soft Spur Press, Missoula, Montana USA
Special funding for
**Soft Spur Chapbooks**
is made by
**Third Ear Productions**

The author gratefully acknowledges the editors of the following journals, in which some of these poems, or earlier versions of them, first appeared:

*Anthology of New England Writers* – "Threshold"

*Arts End Books* – "The Human Condition"

*Black Buzzard Review* – "Light with Dark All Around"

*Caduceus* – "North Shore" (reprinted)

*Ekphrasis* – "While," "Atelier"

*Italian Americana* – "Alannese," "Bus at Dawn," "Cause and Effect,"
"Leaving my Basement Study,"
"Lovers by the Sambre River," "Parkside"

*The Literary Review* – "North Shore"

*New England Jazz History Database* –"Keeping Different Time"(reprinted)

*New Hungers for Old: One-Hundred Years of Italian American Poetry* –
"Cause and Effect" (reprinted)

*96 Inc* – "The Rusted Heart of Henry's Landing (part one)

*The Peralta Press* – "Anonymous Freight," "Somnambulist"

*Sahara* – "'The Rusted Heart of Henry's Landing" (part two)

*Shapes* – "Reciprocal," "Phtygrph," "Shapes"

*Urban Spaghetti* – "Keeping Different Time"

*The Worcester Review* – "Sample"

*The author expresses gratitude to poet* John Surowiecki, *who commented on many of the poems in manuscript, and to* Michael Palma, *poetry editor of Italian Americana, whose support has been invaluable. Thanks to* Valerie Scott *for graphic design assistance, and to* Shaun Gant, *publisher and editor of Soft Spur Press.*

# Contents

For my mother and father
Mary Grace and Edward Anthony Campiglio


And for Denise, Briana, and Andrew

# RECIPROCAL

While I slept, the beach raker came
and combed the area around my blanket.
The lines resemble the grade

of a contour map. Collecting my things,
I become an elevation. Low tide reveals
the long, curved shape of

folded-down marsh grass
which high tide impressed upon it,
as if a giant body had reclined there.

Back home, the face cloth stuck to my toe
in the draining tub is like a rag
of seaweed caught in the undertow.

## ENSEMBLE

Inside the necropolis of a rusty bedspring,
the first grass pokes through caked, blue leaves
beside a white washing machine gleaming
in sunlight that penetrates the canopy.
Nearby, the remains of a swing set creak in the wind,
attended by a spirit of swingers.
The creaking draws me into the speculation
that I've been dumped here, too, that we're
an ensemble of opportunists who've abandoned
traditional function in order to ply transformation—
this dumping ground, our next stage
in the middle of the woods.

## ASHWORTH

It's exactly the sparseness that attracts me
to this off-season beach resort
epitomized by the lone denim woman
walking her Dalmatian down Nudd Ave.
while I hold spurious court from my cheap balcony.
Across the alley, a snipped weathervane
points in all directions at once; the decorated owl
mounted on the gable to scare gulls away
shit on by roof-hopping pigeons.
Opposite the strip's shuttered storefronts
Our Lady of the war-dead memorial
perpetuates Her granite vigil.
My notebook, left open on the sill
last night, has been rained into pulp.

## LIGHT WITH DARK ALL AROUND

I row to an area of moonlight
and cast my line.
Dreaming of a fish dinner,

I reel in a mammal.
It braces itself *on top* of the water,
its eyes beseeching mine.

As it speaks to me in a language
I don't understand, the hook
falls from its mouth.

The rod now feels like a weapon
that's been planted on me.
I let it slip through my hands and sink.

But the animal remains on the surface.
*I don't understand*, I say,
as if it would understand me.

Then quick clouds obscure the moon.
In the dark, I hear the water part;
the chance between us, gone too soon.

## ANONYMOUS FREIGHT

The river and the bridge create a city's cardinal points.
Lying on the floor, I orient the *x* and *y* of me
and plot the freight train's slow advance
by approximating the location of its sound

according to the names of the streets it passes.
Heading east into the city limits, the train
fades west to my room, and I fade with it
into registers I can't hear or name—

it, a weightless
sentience
in space
that rejoins

the tracks
in my palms,
which I plant on the floor
to get back on my feet

while the last of the train
passes through me.

# THE RUSTED HEART OF HENRY'S LANDING

1

Armed with quahog shells
I dig into the tidal flat and bed down.

This is my take on the *disinterested passions.*
And you reciprocate in due time with the wave

that falls into this open grave
and deposits on my chest

a heart-shaped stone, a piece
of rust, an old potato chip.


2

The headlights of traffic along Bourne Ave.
light up the salt marsh and run off my dark wall,

projecting the spaces between towels
hanging on the clothesline out back—

lucid, discontinuous cuts of ghost fabric
that pass over my skin and dry me to a chill.

## CAUSE AND EFFECT

Camped outside the door,
the persistent stray that insists on a home
charges the opening.

Although I stop the cat with both hands
it keeps coming and gets through my legs.

The commotion doesn't seem to bother my father.
He's in the kitchen, his respite from the dead.
He looks younger since he died

and doesn't say a word,
wiping the counter top dry.

Then a car pulls into the driveway
and the tires crackle on the gravel.
I scamper outside, but there's only

the cat triumphant in the window,
my father neatly squaring the kitchen rag.

## NEIGHBORS

After Leo secures his exit
with a clink of the chain-link gate,
starlings feast on the freshly turned

worms of his potato patch.
The visible leads to the vision

that reforms the water of my eyes:
the flock in unison shifts
along the mounds of earth,

like a blanket pulled across
a row of sleeping bodies.

His water-stained bathtub
full of rainwater reflects the sky.
Leaf-scar—what bug has got my basil?

## KEEPING DIFFERENT TIME

A line of improbable cars
wheels through the neighborhood
on an egg of light
without rail or clatter.
Tracks of broken snow
connect the yards
beyond the ravine.
With branches slapping
against my coat,
I climb closer to read
the freight names—
evasive evidence
gone along a crack of light.

## PHTYGRPH

The playground is animated by the wind
that becomes animated
as it sways the trees.

I'm a grown man on a swing,
late at night, a luminous ebb and flow.
I see through the bark and into the vein

that draws the earth closer to the sky.
We circulate sap or blood, grow branches
or limbs; tree-head, head of hair, flung by the wind.

## BUS AT DAWN

Seated before the pagoda
I follow its pyramidal form
bending in a visionary breeze.

Floors dislodging corridors
send empty rooms free—
the pagoda, seated before me.

What breeze? There's only the vision
revealing more of itself. Leaving
Chinatown, I head toward

South of Market—a body of
standing ash, mind of formless heat
at a MUNI stop. The approaching sign

in the crown of the 14 Mission
shoots the gray sky with tiny yellows.
We are of one light, boarding the bus

and riding to a gamut of ill-suited jobs
or not, while the involuntary
life in us all hums along.

# SHAPES

Boarding the *vaporetto* at San Marco
we taxi into overcast water
and pass a hearse-boat
headed for the cemetery island
of San Michele.

Adding to the black austerity
is a fleet of mourners,
followed by their bright cargo
of flowers.

We get off at Murano
and watch the glassblowers
bake and blow out the bodies
of lamps, vases, figurines,
with the breath of Vesta herself.

O to be tooled and crafted like that!
To be made into something desirable
to someone who'd like to take me home.
To be made that fragile.

# OLD PHILADELPHIA

With the urge to conjure and experience
what my father was like as a young man
I return to his old immigrant neighborhood

in a dream. Walking along a seemingly endless
Italian street, I reach an incongruously situated
English pub. After I order a drink, a very drunk,
very non-Italian man asks me what my name is.

When I tell him, he begins to ridicule
the long string of vowels. We fight
and spill into the street. He draws a knife,

which is actually a letter opener. I knock it free
and kick it into the storm drain. His will goes slack.
*Fait accompli*. Then the bartender brings me
an envelope that fell out of my pocket

during the fight, and which I don't recall carrying.
Labeled "Family History," it's folded and sealed
in intricate ways. I need that opener back!

## NORTH SHORE

Off the shoulder of a rural stretch of Rt. 95
near the Groveland/Georgetown exit

my father has parked his car,
missing the driveway by a long shot.
He wakes early in his own bed (I haven't slept)

and returns to his vehicle as a matter of course—
the distance between points apparently negligible.

As he begins to drive away, I'm right there with him,
running in the breakdown lane after him, pleading
*You don't drive anymore!* Curious about my panic

he slows his speed enough to encourage my pursuit of him.
When he adjusts the side view mirror for a better look,

our eyes connect like guardrail down that highway.
Then he becomes visibly agitated and begins to accelerate,
two, three years late for work.

## WORD SPEED

Meeting a friend at the bus station
for a parting farewell, I'm earlier
than I need to be, and the experience
of waiting changes me.

With a rash desire for travel myself
I inquire about departures to Boston
but mistakenly say, *To Worcester*
and the clerk replies

*You are in Worcester.*
Taken aback, I chuckle and tell her
*Oh, I'm sorry, I'm still awake, I mean asleep*
and take a schedule back to my breakfast table
where I begin reading instead the classified section

of the newspaper, and realize that this isn't Worcester
nor Boston. It's Missoula, Montana.
I'm enrolled in a graduate writing program
and arrived well before the start of school

to find a place to live. That's what I'm early for,
I think. But wait—no—I abandoned that program
years ago and have since moved back home.
It's my friend who's in transit. I'm here

to see her off. Still, that can't be right either,
because she's long become a stranger
and so I don't know her plans anymore.
Therefore, it must be the past when
I still knew her. And if that's true

then I could very well be traveling myself
because I hardly go anywhere
anymore in the present.

## SAMPLE

On the blank TV screen, the white door's reflection.

Sunlight leans against the exercise bike,
as if to say, "I've come 93 million miles
before taking this rest—what have you done?"
I admit that my interest is vagabond,
that my goals are the multiplicity
of a vagrant soul. Outside in the heat,

white, bulb-shaped blossoms the size of baby heads,
and polygonal, like miniature geodesic domes,
emit a foul smell—a brief visual and nasal display
that contrasts the mild, long-standing weed.

Wandering downtown, I notice life stirring
from the three-dimensional lettering
on the bank's textured façade.
Inside its capital "B" are upper and lower bird's nests.
They're like bunk beds or the berths on a train,
a two-family home or one extended one—

indeed, an alphabet functioning on multi-levels.

Later in the day, my fellow diner,
setting a pair of scissors beside his plate,
uses cut-up and collage to retool
the Chinese zodiac printed on his place mat,

then tells me to wipe my mouth—there's a poem on my napkin.

## THE CLOWN

Tossing three bowling pins
the clown juggles one and two
but number three continues to rise.

He keeps juggling one and two
while lunging for number three
but number three juggles him into the air
and he disappears

as one, two and three fall to the ground.
The audience cheers, and then they, too, are gone.
Sometime afterward, when the clown returns

to collect his pins, the ground suddenly opens
into running water and they wash away.
Unruffled, he stoops by the bank for a drink
as one, two and three reappear upstream

and float toward him. Without understanding why
he knows at that instant he must choose between
gathering his pins before they disappear for good

or satisfying his thirst before the stream
juggles the water down to nothing.
He stoops by the bank and chooses.

## SOMNAMBULIST

Leaning his ladder against the backyard tree
he climbs into the green night
and whispers to the leaves—
each one, an ear.

At the top, he pauses to admire
his grounds like never before.

*And what shall I love if not enigma?*

When he comes down, he crosses the dark yard—
a wind among winds—climbs the stairs
of his house, and returns to his room.

Seated at the edge of the bed
he grips the broom like an oar
and working it into the ocean of the floor
sets off to inspect his more distant properties.

# LOVERS BY THE SAMBRE RIVER

*—after René Magritte's* Les Amants

She leaves her house
in the middle of the night
and heads for the nearby river.

At the edge of the bridge, she stands
in perfect balance with her derangement,
the night sky, and the swirling current,
allowing for the chance to reconsider her intent.

It is perhaps the most fulfilling moment
of her life as she decides to jump.
He's entranced by a vision of where she last stood.

When she's pulled from the water, her nightgown's
wrapped around her face like a falconer's hood.

# THE FUTURE IS A CUT-UP

*—after William S. Burroughs*


If there is no transmigration of souls
then I contradict myselves.
The words of a text reappear
in their next context as a cut-up poem.
If the earth itself has a soul
when it transmigrates, where do you think it'd go?
*We're all here to go*, says Mr. Burroughs.

The sentence and its imposition
on the shape and will of the mind—
no wonder it also refers to a jail term.
Therefore, meet the oppression in substance,
treat the material of words, cut, and rearrange—
*at the point of intersection, the future leaks out,*
Burroughs interjects in the present.

# CONTEMPLATING THE ENIGMA

*—after Giorgio de Chirico's* The Mystery and Melancholia of a Street

The arcade suggests a structural enclosure, but there is no back to the building—only sculpted shade.

Its bright façade is a hybrid of classical architecture and modern factory, connecting the foreground to its vanishing point.

In one corner of the piazza, a circus wagon has been unloaded. One can't be sure if this happened a couple hours or several years ago.

Nearby, a child rolls her hula-hoop toward the light, searching for signs that the circus may still be in town.

Beyond the statue of the famous philosopher, whose shadow leans toward the girl, a network of alleys leads the pedestrian to a legendary gallery with its collection of Italian Metaphysical paintings.

He gravitates toward *The Mystery and Melancholia of a Street* and enters its framed cityscape, from where he follows the sharp perspective of the arcade to its vanishing point … and vanishes with it.

# BITE TO EAT

*—after Max Ernst*

Menus are being passed around a café
that has remained open despite construction
and the smell of paint and plaster.
Each collage-like menu is unique—
proof that the chef is some sort of wizard.
Although there isn't any food on the tables
nor visible wait staff, the act of meditating on the collages
seems to stir the customers into other forms of satiation.
I take a seat at the counter, and while waiting for service,

make a rubbing of the wood-grained top
with my napkin and pencil. The patrons
to my left and right magically appear in the *frottage*.
But when I look up at them, they're phantoms.
Then the café itself loses its trappings
and I'm in an art studio belonging to Max Ernst.
His trademark "sun-and-moon eclipse" adorns the transom.
There's a monograph of the artist on the counter and I open to:

*… makes a Rhineland forest out of the edges of wallpaper ….*

I repeat the words aloud until the phrase achieves the power
of an incantation, and M.E. steps out from behind a canvas
where the *decalcomania* of a forest is still wet.
Then handing me his latest collage, he explains
that it's assembled like a menu, with the illustrations
depicting his appetite for a variety of artistic techniques.

The texts and images serve as ingredients for the vessel
of my body that begins to function alembic-like.
Heated by the divine, I rise and fall, One with All.
In the process, the master metamorphoses
into a phantom, and I'm counter-side in the café again,
passing my menu onto the next patron.

# WIG SALON

Rows of wigs on busts are tiered like a crowd to scale
inside the storefront window of Sonja's Salon.
Some of the heads, partially painted with a speckled eye
or showy brow, contrast like aliens on display.

Truncated hands reach out from the nails boutique next door;
a tailor's mannequin, dressed to the nines, preens
to passers-by; legless shoes step out from the shadows
of a cobbler's shop. The spirit could assemble and animate
a body right here in this block of self-enhancement.

Studying my face in the window, I find the *flâneur* in me
displaced to Boulevard de Strasbourg nearly 100 years
in the past, experiencing in real time Eugène Atget's
sidewalk shot of *Corsets.* The headless automata
are stirred into life by dreaming through them….

Then I'm back to Worcester's Franklin Street,
and turning to the shopper beside me, invite her
up to my room for some mutual enhancement
before we both return to the scrap heap.

# TRAKL, SPRUNG

*—after Georg Trakl*

A pharmacist by trade, the poet self-dispenses
for his addiction. Unfinished drafts of poems
trouble his mind. His finished poems (which he
obsessively rewrites in his quest for a perfection

that does not exist in language) trouble my mind.
With the outbreak of World War One, he's assigned
to a medical unit at the front where the carnage
that he witnesses triggers a nervous breakdown

and he's transferred to a military hospital
for psychiatric observation. After a failed attempt
by his friend, von Ficker, to secure the poet's release
Trakl, resourceful pharmacist to the end,

having stashed an ample supply of cocaine,
administers his own release. The drug state serves
as a demilitarized zone between beyond and return.
And then, he's exclusively beyond.

One of his last poems spoke
about the "unborn generation"
but as a symbol of loss, hope,
or more desperation?

# WHILE

—*after René Magritte's* The Explanation

While drunkenly groping in the overgrown garden at night
for the bottle of liquor that you hid there
you mistakenly pull a carrot from the ground.

Sobered by this reversal, and enthralled
by the vegetable's mineral replacement of organic matter
you display the prize on your mantelpiece.

While admiring your unusual harvest, you detect
a subtle volatility within the petrifaction:
an organic replacement of mineral matter.

Throughout the night, the prize undergoes gradations
between a carrot-shaped bottle of vegetable juice
and a bottle-shaped carrot of glassy root.

It is both man-made and a product of the stars
from the bottom of the bottle to the tip of the carrot
while moonlight brightens the new hole in the old garden.

# ATELIER

—*after M.C. Escher's* Reptiles

The potted soil sprinkled with a few natural laws
could be a microcosm of the earth.

Suddenly fertile and open to further conjecture
he arranges his paper and pencils and unleashes
a reptilian line that emerges from the tessellated pulp
and comes to life with expert draftsmanship—

the life cycle of an alligator-to-scale, extended
up and off the pad and across the desk paraphernalia.
The elder adult pauses at the highest point
with a puff of smoke—

a reflective summation of *crocodilus*—
before returning to its previous state
as the subject of a flat study,

only to begin again its ascent into spatial dimensions.
Having set his cyclical vision in perpetual motion,
the artist, now superfluous to the art,
withdraws beyond his tools and ideation.

# ETERNAL ART

*—after Max Ernst*

They once grew crown to crown, swaying in the breeze.

Cut down and planed into planks, they were transfigured into artifice.

Their spirit untouched, the trees now sway in the heart of the city through the woodwork of certain rooms, buildings and façades.

One of these places is a gallery whose current exhibition is a series of forests by Max Ernst, on which I've based a series of poems, entitled *Forernsts.*

As I stand before one of the trees, a breeze through the window stirs the work into life, or stirs me into stirring the work into life—a brush with the wild in the heart of the city.

Standing crown to crown with the other viewers in the gallery, I'm part of a multiplicity of interpretation. Soon we're an animated crowd, swaying in the breeze.

# THE HUMAN CONDITION

*—after René Magritte's* La Condition humaine

The easel is positioned in front of the window
just so, so that what's painted on the canvas
portrays from a viewer's perspective
what would be in the landscape
without the painting there.

The proposition here is that the canvas
also covers up what's behind the easel
like a word that eclipses the object it denotes.

Step to one side and the perspective changes.
Clear the obstacle, and the window's in the way.
Go outside, and I find myself in the way.
*Clear the self*, the artist says, and artifice falls away.

# DEINSTITUTIONALIZED

She rubs the coins
together in her hand
as if something further
were contained in the metal.

Her face almost changes
into an expression of thanks.
But then her invisible team of huskies

(and so I must see them, too)
yanks at the toy reins
in her other hand,
and the empty collars come alive.

She lurches forward
with playful banter
and trots to other customers

in the snowy, fast-food
lunchtime parking lot
before steering her sled
into line at the drive-thru.

## LEAVING MY BASEMENT STUDY

Late, I feel my way out
from the dark basement,
groping for the next operative word.

Caught in a curl of linoleum
the irregular door swings

by its own weight—
the house, still settling after
nine decades and five generations.

Moonlight flits through fast clouds—
tonight's work in hand—muddy flagstones—
cleaning off my bare feet in the wet grass.

# THE ROLLING GROUNDS OF THE FRONTIER

The cows graze off the postcard.
The postcard flies off the spinner rack.

*Façade* derives from *faccia*, Italian for face—
the face of a building—
how does it look to ... or at ... you?

In the day room, a man shadow-boxes,
stepping and bobbing around chairs.

His jabs and hooks assail the air.
Then he clenches a potted floor plant
and the sport goes out of him.

Spinner racks with yellow flowers
become a mullein field. The flowers seed

perennial sympathy cards. At the edge
of the field, the face of the building turns inward

and watches the man return to his bed.
He remembers a time when Route 9
was a carriage trail with a cow crossing,

becomes disoriented when he can't remember
that *mucca* is Italian for cow. Flipping further

through his spinner rack of memory,
he winces when the hinges creak.
The mullein's biennial surge dies back and withers.

He's the stalk of a man; the gift shop,
closed for renovations.

## PARKSIDE

With my door ajar
I'm a wave of a body

napping on the floor.
The surf of me circulates

through alleys with ceilings of fog.
At times I reach the storm drain

or swell toward street signs
unreadable in the fog. The woman

who's coming to visit me, illicitly,
decides to turn around.

## THRESHOLD

The evocative arises from the rub
of a double negative:
out-of-business in the off-season,
the motel between hands,

the plentiful vacancy of it all.
Overrunning empty umbrella stands
a community of dandelions—

brilliant heads bobbing off the rocky neck.
High tide claims the narrow beach
in the quick dark.

The moon in one quadrant
of the mullioned window.
The rising moon. The dead square.
The circle is where clouds travel.

Across my kitchen floor
a surf of garlic skins.

## THE HEART OF THE LANDSCAPE

White water guts the mountain.
The strewn heart
of the mountain constructs
the river bed.

The bed carries the heart to me
in pieces. I, too, am gutted
by the impulse to write this poem.

Downstream, back home—
storm debris cruises through
the bird bath, like stirred-up
leaves in the tea pot.

## DARKRIVER

A James Joyce devotee friend of mine practices
her cello beside the Clark Fork River tonight.
Her song incorporates the sounds

of water on rock, breeze
through the hollow body,

the presence of Anna Livia Plurabelle.
We're strung across evanescent frets—
the bones of our inner ears, vibrating!

## MAIN SOUTH TROUPE

The sidewalk of Castle Street is strewn with the trash
of Main Street. The suit from city hall
doesn't know where to park.

He has all of our names in his briefcase.
We have the element of surprise.
An eroded fence post protrudes from a green bush.
The gray wood tip of it could be a bird.

A bird lands there and the fence tip flies away.
The local ornithologist has no record

of these gray wooden birds. The local anthropologist,
however, has documented arcane instances
in which aged wood became animate.
Meanwhile, the suit from city hall has a mandate

to sort out our interchangeable apartment numbers.
The wind, fauna-like, reverses itself, and the trash
of Castle Street shifts toward the corner of Main Street.

# THE ASIAN INSTITUTE

In the alley behind the bar
a blues riff trembles
through a trash can cover.

Prayers flags on the rotary clothesline.
Jumbled, coexisting neighborhoods
on this precious peninsular.

Opposite the park
the Chinese pagoda's
fluid yet comprehensive

architecture is particle space
made macroscopic, that which
is already present simply revealed.

The microscopic dance that holds forth
within my seated body sinks into enzymes,
rises into pyramidal form.

## WEATHERED

With elegant
tenacity
cordgrass

and beach rose
supplant
the foot path.

Keen on trends
my father once told me
that I missed the boat

but he was only half-right
when I pulled up my oars
and just wanted to float.

## TALL FLOOR MODEL

The steamed mirror sweats out the face
I drew the bath before. I study the lines
then wipe them clean. But the face grows

its way back, planted in the glass
looking for *his* reflection, wanting
to know his position in the world.
And this gives rise to a host of considerations

multiplying in the mirror, in contrast
to the tall floor model down the hall
that stands so remote with no one there.

The stairway to my apartment smells of decades
of smoke and booze. Baggy, blue drawstrings.
Mail key in hand. Fresh rejections.
My pants on the iced-over clothesline

resemble carcasses hanging from meat hooks.
Toilet for a poor man's retreat; advance with the book.
In the Christian statue shop down the street

shelves crowded with the Jesus icon
draw shoppers of a like mind, like a mob.

## ALANNESE

Standing with my older second cousin outside his house on Via Prati
in Alanno, I think of how we've lived a tale of elder siblings.
My side went the way of steerage. And I'm still adrift,
grandson of the sister who emigrated.

*Ala,* wing; *-ese,* suffix denoting one's place of origin—
on the Alannese coat of arms, a wing, representing the diverse
migratory bird population along the Pescara River's rich vegetation.

Although my mother was born here, I'm a tourist surveying my own
roots. But I have the good fortune of arriving during the harvest
celebration of *Madonna delle Grazie* and *San Biagio.*

For tonight's festivities, a custom-made cast of the Maiden of the Hills,
girded by a pyrotechnic framework, including a roman candle
protruding from each bosom, stands ready;

her regional costume, altered to match the Italian flag
and crowning the figure, the distinctive, two-handled copper water pot
as traditionally carried on top of the head.

With the band playing popular Abruzzese music, a lit fuse
to the ornamental Maiden initiates an elaborate succession of fireworks
and the dancer inside the hollow prop performs the *Ballo della pupa.*

In the bright, smoky climax of the *festa,* how the apparatus—
and the tourist in me—disappear! The Maiden swirls
across the piazza. Colorful sparks fly off her body.
A spectacle for dark hills.

# NOTES

*Ashworth.* Ashworth-by-the-Sea, a hotel/restaurant in Hampton Beach, NH.

*The Rusted Heart of Henry's Landing.* A rental house near Moody Beach, Wells, ME.

*Bus at Dawn.* MUNI is San Francisco's "muni"cipal public transit system; 14 Mission, the city bus that runs the length of the Mission District connecting to downtown.

*Shapes.* Vaporetto is a taxi-boat shuttling commuters between the Venetian lagoon islands. San Marco is the major island; Murano, a smaller one, famous for glass-blowing. Vesta: Roman god of the hearth.

*North Shore.* Eastern part of Massachusetts north of Boston.

*The Clown.* In memory of Peter Abbott, a Worcester, MA-based mime and clown who died in Europe while touring with a circus.

*Somnambulist.* "And what shall I love if not the enigma?" from Giorgio de Chirico (1888-1978), Greek-born, Italian pre-Surrealist, renowned for his "Metaphysical" paintings.

*Lovers by the Sambre River.* René Magritte (1898-1967), Belgian Surrealist painter and theoretician. In this painting (*The Lovers* in English), the faces of a couple embracing are covered by cloth or sacks, an image associated with the story of the suicide of Magritte's mother, who drowned herself in the Sambre River near Magritte's boyhood home.

*The Future Is a Cut-Up.* Quotes are from William S. Burroughs (1914-1997), American expatriate writer who promoted Brion Gyson's "cut-up" method of textual production. *Bite to Eat.* Max Ernst (1891-1976), German Dadaist and Surrealist painter, sculptor, and graphic artist and early, core member of French Surrealism, who later left the movement, as Magritte did. Frottage: pencil rubbing of an object placed beneath paper and moved for multiple effects. Decalcomania: pressing paper or glass over paint on a canvas and reworking the textural alteration. Quote and monograph reference from *Max Ernst: Life and Work* by John Russell.

*Wig Salon.* Eugène Atget (1857-1927), French photographer who documented Parisian architecture and street scenes.

*Trakl, Sprung.* Georg Trakl (1887-1914), Austrian-born Expressionist poet, whose last months of life inspired this poem. Ludwig von Ficker was Trakl's editor and friend.

*Atelier.* M.C. Escher (1898-1972), Dutch graphic artist and lithographer.

*Eternal Art.* After Ernst's forest motif. "Forernsts" is created specifically for the poem. *Parkside.* An ocean district in San Francisco.

*Darkriver.* James Joyce (1882-1941), Irish expatriate writer who progressed from traditional forms to *Finnegans Wake* featuring matriarchal Anna Livia Plurabelle. Anna Livia, a represention of Dublin's River Liffey. Plurabelle, derived from Italian for "loveliest." Last line inspired by Etheridge Knight (1931 – 1991), African-American avant-garde poet whose first book was written in prison.

*Alannese.* Alanno is an Italian hill town in the Abruzzo region, Pescara Province. Madonna della Grazie: patron saint of Alanno (in English, Our Lady of the Graces), also the name of its renaissance church, built to venerate a miraculous apparition of the Madonna; San Biagio: a patron saint (in English, St. Blaise), celebrated for the "Blessing of the Throats"; Ballo della pupa: Dance of the Doll.

A full descendant from the Italian region of Abruzzo (where his surname is **Campilii**), **STEPHEN CAMPIGLIO** was born in Stoneham, Massachusetts and raised in the Merrimack River Valley. He earned a B.A. in English from Worcester State College and M.A. in Education from Assumption College. A longtime resident of Worcester, MA, he has also lived in Boston, San Francisco, Missoula, MT, and Portland, OR. He now makes his home in southern Worcester County.

Stephen has served as an arts organizer for decades, including as a member of *Noh Place Artists' Cooperative* in Worcester; co-founder of *Second Wind Reading Series* in Missoula, MT; founder/coordinator of *Borders Poetry Reading Series* in Framingham, MA; co-founder/co-coordinator of the *d'Alzon Arts Series* at Assumption College; and founder of the *Mishi-maya-gat Spoken Word & Music Series* at Manchester Community College in Manchester, CT, which he continues to coordinate. Stephen was a featured poet in *Italian Americana* and a finalist in the *Bordighera Poetry Book Prize*. He has performed his poetry in a multitude of settings over the years, including with the spoken word bands*, Forbidden Poets* and more recently, *Cross-Fluence (*formerly,*The Bluebottles).*

*Photo of the Author*